MW00817754

Not
Seen
But
Recognized

A
Little
Knowledge
Is
Dangerous!

was Read
2-7-11

Elijah Muhammad, Messenger of Allah

SECRETARIUS - iii

THE SECRETS OF FREEMASONRY

SECRETARIUS - V

THE
SECRETS
OF
FREEMASONRY

BY
ELIJAH MUHAMMAD
MESSENGER OF ALLAH

Published by
Secretarius MEMPS Publications
P.O. Box 162412 ● Atlanta, GA 30321
Wholesale & Distribution (770) 907-2212
Email: admin@elijahmuhammadbooks.com
www.elijahmuhammadbooks.com

The Secrets of Freemasonry

Copyright © 1994
Secretarius MEMPS Publications
First Printing 1994
Second Printing 1997
Third Printing 2002

All rights reserved.
No part of this book may be reproduced
in any form, except for the inclusion of
brief quotations in reviews, without
permission in writing from the
author/publisher.

ISBN 1-884855-05-9

Printed in the United States of America

ACKNOWLEDGEMENT

It is with the assistance of Allah (God), Master Fard Muhammad, and that of His Last and Greatest Messenger, Elijah Muhammad, that we, Secretarius, put forth this humble effort. I'd like to thank the Secretarius Staff for their tireless work and commitment. I pray that Allah blesses them to benefit greatly from their contribution.

As-Salaam-Alaikum

Nasir Makr Hakim, Founder
SECRETARIUS MEMPS

INTRODUCTION

"We must become aware of the knowledge of self and the time in which we are living. You must know these things whether you agree that Elijah Muhammad is on time or out of time. If what I say is out of season, it goes for nothing. If I am on time or in season, then all I say will bear fruit."

The Most Honorable Elijah Muhammad,
Last Messenger of Allah -to you all.

It has been revealed by the Honorable Elijah Muhammad, Last Messenger of Allah, that the histories of the Holy Qur'an and Bible are used to teach us, Black people, the true knowledge of our history. The truths in each of these books have, in most cases, been hidden from the eyes and ears of most; consequently, a lack of knowledge has been prevalent among our people and as the scriptures themselves bear witness: "My people are destroyed for the lack of knowledge."

The following passage is lifted from Edwin R. Embree's book, "Brown American," printed in 1946, page 54, which Messenger Elijah Muhammad cited in his book, "Message To The Blackman In America," wherein it stated that, "He, [Mr. Embree] quotes a devil, (whiteman) Henry Berry, as saying while speaking in the Virginia House of Delegates in 1832 and describing the situation as existed at that time in many parts of the South: 'We have as far as possible, closed every avenue by which light may enter the slaves' mind ... If we could extinguish the capacity to see the light, our work would be complete; they would then be on a level with the beast of the field and we should be safe.'"

The above cite is not only chosen to testify of the degree to which this government or its founding fathers of this country went, to kill our capacity to be educated, but it also shows that whoever the speaker was talking to, in addition to himself, used jargon or terminology common to men of higher knowledge. Men of higher knowledge use the term "light" to describe knowledge not common to the common man. Many of the founding fathers of this country were, and still are, high degree Masons and Shriners. They have sworn oaths not to reveal, what they call, secrets. It just so happen that the "secrets" they are bound by oaths to keep secret, just happen to be the truths to free you and I from our grave of ignorance. In the above passage, they weren't voting or deliberating on whether or not the truth was going to be revealed, they were deliberating on how to destroy our capacity to see light at all - ever.

Even with the accomplishment of Prince Hall, Blacks were still somewhat short changed, because even though they had some knowledge, what they had was mostly speculative symbolism. That means, they were able to use signs among themselves and enjoyed a minimal elevation over their common brother, but white Masons didn't respect them and hated to refer to a black Mason as a brother. The Honorable Elijah Muhammad pointed out that the first three degrees of Masonry were the answer to their slavery, but how many of them understood that and have demonstrated a significant work to prove it? The white man gave it to blacks, but the applicable elements were gutted out; therefore, the black man could only use it for so-called social status, privileges or a "key to the city."

Many have wondered and even marveled over just what Masonry is and many more are somewhat hard pressed for a description, but that doesn't mean it's indescribable. Within the scriptures, Holy Qur'an and Bible, which houses most of the symbolism used by Masons, are symbolic stories echoed many times and are talking about the same thing. Many prophets acted out different scenarios which were only signs of what was to come in this time, but due to a lack of knowledge, many modern day Black Masons fall short when trying to apply a symbolic meaning to reality. This is what made the Honorable Elijah stand out so boldly.

He was able to demonstrate works beyond what any man is known for. The symbolism in the scripture dealing with an architect being killed and his body being lost, was a sign, the seal of which was broken by the Honorable Elijah Muhammad. Not only did he teach the knowledge, wisdom and understanding on this matter, he also demonstrated the fulfillment of it. He told the world that it wasn't his knowledge, and rightly so, judging by what the white legislators stated, he said he got it from Allah (God) Who had come, as the scripture as well as the symbolism in Masonry testifies to: That the searchers found the dead man, but couldn't lift him. Like Marcus Garvey: he tried to help the poor slave in America, who was mentally dead, but history shows that Garvey didn't have the right grip, but as the scripture teaches that God had to go Himself and show them how to raise a dead man. So it was. The Honorable Elijah Muhammad lifted the Blackman in America up in such a way that the world knows it had to have been God who taught him how to take hold of a dead man.

It was Elijah Muhammad who has revealed more to black Masons than any white Mason would ever teach them. It was this mighty Messenger who told and prove to them the true interpretation of Hiram, who was hit in the head and taken West; yet, it wasn't until God, Allah, in the Person of Master Fard Muhammad, raised him from the dead to a living perpendicular.

It's time that we know the truth, regardless of how secret it has become; it is time.

Minister Nasir Makr Hakim
C.E.O., Secretarius Publications

Table of Contents

A TRUE MASON

As-Salaam-Alaikum: I am Elijah Muhammad, the preacher of freedom, justice and equality, to you, my dear people, who has been in the Western Hemisphere, in America for four hundred long years. And now the day has arrived that you must turn to your own: Your own God and your people, that you may be able to see the Hereafter.

The Hereafter means after the holy war or after Armageddon or after the war between Satan and Almighty God. This is what's meant when we say the hereafter. It means after the war between right and wrong has been fought. This war is often called a war between God and the devil. The devil seeks to hold supremacy over God, since he has ruled the people for six thousand (6,000) years, he desires to continue to try to holding his place as a ruler of the people and seeks to bring before the people every opposition that he possibly can to destroy their hearts and their minds toward the worship and obedience to Almighty God, Allah.

Here in the Western Hemisphere, in America, where there is 22 million original black people living, whose fathers suffered slavery for around three hundred long years, and this enslavement of our fathers has caused us to believe in the enemy or adversary of God, the real devil himself. It is hard today to get our people to disbelieve in the devil and believe in Almighty God, because they never knew anything of God or the devil, only by the teachings of the slave-master and the slave-master was always careful to conceal himself so that they might not know who he is; therefore, it was impossible for them to learn who was God and who was the devil.

These are really two Gods. The devil is a God himself, as mentioned by Jesus in the New Testament, that he is the god of this world, the prince of the power of hell. This is true that the devil has been the ruler for six thousand years and God of this world. "This world" means the world of the devil. Under his rule the people forget the real True God and the way to that True God, because he will not teach the people.

Again, the parable of the vine or the olive tree, pardon me, the fig tree, that Jesus, as the book say, cursed, was also a sign of this world that this world has never produced converts to the will of Almighty God Allah. Never has any so-called American Negro been taught by white people to believe in Almighty God Allah and his true religion Islam. Only in higher organizations or we say Masonry, in the Masonics, there is a little teachings at the top mostly of this particular order that mentions the teachings of Almighty God Allah. But you have to pay a lot of money to become a 33rd degree Mason; therefore, you are an absolute victim, as Isaiah teaches you, that you buy that which does not bring you any gain. To buy that kind of teachings does not gain you the hereafter. We must have something that is pure. A Mason cannot be a good Mason unless he knows the Holy Qur'an and follows its teaching. This book is the only book that will make a true Mason. The Bible won't make you a true one. I say, if you are a true Moslem friend, then alright, lets have it in the open and not in the secret.

These things I warn you who are listening, that the time is right now and is at hand, that everything, everything of good or bad must be made known. We are living in the end of this world, the judgment of this world. These are the days of judgment mentioned in the Bible as in the days of the judgment or in the days of the resurrection of the dead; these days represent years and not just little 24 hour days as we know them today, but they mean years. In the years of the judgment, or the resurrection of the dead, we are in those days now. The coming of Allah and the teachings of Islam to we, who have been lost from our kind, native land and our country for the past 400 years, mean the judgment. God doesn't come until the judgment or until the end of the world of Satan. As you have it written in the Bible, prophesied throughout the Bible and also absolutely mentioned in Thessalonians, that God comes after the working of Satan, the devil. And after he has done all that he possibly can do of evil, then God comes after allowing him to go to the poor or giving him the freedom to try and take all the people with him to hell if possible.

These are the days now that we are living in. I want you to understand me dear people. You are not in the actual way of the truth, you have not actually believed it. Your time now has come that even if you would just turn to Almighty God, you would enjoy salvation or heaven in this world, and in the hereafter you are assured of the heaven. But even in this life, God gives the righteous peace of mind and contentment. He is the protector of the righteous after He makes His appearance and religion that the judgment will come and there will be a great separation at the judgment. This is true, but you don't believe that you are living in this time, that there is a great separation now in the workings.

When you first heard that there was someone in your midst giving names similar to foreign names or Indians names, such as Karriem, Biarh, Muhammad, Farrakhan, Hassan, Hasim, Ali, and many names that you now hear being given to your own people and they being called by these names, you're so dead to the knowledge of self, kind, truth and the true God, that you not only don't pay any attention to them, but even make fun of these names, because you never heard of these names before. Instead of grabbing a dictionary to see what certain names mean, you're consequently called foolish or fools in the Bible and the Holy Qur'an. You would learn that these names mean good names of God. As mentioned in mostly all the teachings of religion, God has 99 names and the 100th is Allah, which mean all the names of good, and will be saved.

These people, it is true, if they hold fast and does not loose their salvation by hating to hear the real truth of them, they will be removed out of the area where there will be war between God and the devil. It's only the people who opposes God that God will fight and bring to a naught. It is not the people who do not oppose God and do not teach other people to oppose Him, but it is that vicious and evil people who teaches against the belief in Almighty God and teaches other people to hate those who believe in Almighty God Allah. These are the people who receives severe judgments of God and I warn you my people, since I see that you don't understand too well, that you should come to the knowledge of the truth. [1]

WHICH ONE WILL SURVIVE THE WAR OF ARMAGEDDON?

Which one will survive the war of Armageddon, which is now taking place? We're going into that war and we're in it now this very minute. If you believe Christianity, which has mistreated you and hung you on trees, then I think you should look at this and think well. If a murderer will survive peace, which we have experienced all our lives, the heavens do not give us no trouble. But we disobey the laws, rules of the heavens, which obeys the Creator. The Star and the Moon and the Sun obeys the law of it's creator, but this stuff over here, stars and stripes (see page 7) to our left is the made up of an enemy against that to our right. He is opposed to the laws that govern that which he cannot do without himself. He cannot find no place to live, but in the peaceful kingdom of the universe. Regardless to how he boasts, he can't build one out side of it. Let him try and build him a universe, then he can be independent of ours. Since he was not able to build him a universe, then obey the laws of ours. That he can't do, because one of our Black scientists, a little over six thousand, six hundred years ago, made him according to his wish. He didn't make him according to our wish. He made him according to his wish.

This trouble maker was made of the nature of making trouble. When his God made him, He made him and he said to him, after he had made him, "Go to now, and make all of the mischief that you can before the coming of the Mahdi." Who is the Mahdi? [He] is the God we call Allah and we call him other names, but He is the One also that is referred to as the Son of Man in the Bible that will come. Mahdi means a name of Self Independence. The Man Who doesn't rely on others. He's Self Independent and He's One that is coming in the last day to bring about the judgment of the made man, and He's referred to by many as being the Son of Man.

The Son of Man is that man Who is given authority and power by God to carry out His judgment upon the people. That's what the Son of Man does. It goes on also for the Mahdi being born out of His nation by a woman that is not of His nation. But the man that produced the child, that she give birth to, was of us, Black man. He married her to get an unlike child so that he could send that child among our people and his people to produce a ruler of us who were lost among the unalike people. The man he made from among his people, and the enemy, was and is the God of the judgment and destruction of the unalike people, who has attracted us for these last 6,000 years to follow them. Unalike is the white people; they are unalike us, and we are not like them and they are not like us, only in the [form] of a man, [and not by nature]. That's why they calls him mankind, because he's just kind of like the real man, but he's not the real one.

God is able to fulfill His promise to us. He has come and offered you that Flag on the right (sun, moon, & star), which means that it is time now to rule your own, that's your own, and He has offered it to us. We have a song we sing of that beauty like this: "Allah has given to us, our own, the Sun Moon and Star for a Flag." I don't think you will find the white people running all over the earth with that on their head, because they know better; they don't have part in it; they have time in it, but not part of the creation. When you ask the white man about his secret order call Masonry or Masonic, he want you to answer that you were not made in that, but you were born in that. That is true. We are born Muslims and cannot be accepted by saying I was made a Muslim. We were created Muslims. [2]

Islam is not a religion. We call it a religion, but it's not a religion, because it is the nature of us; therefore, the nature of us can't be called a religion. That's why the 30th chapter and the 30th verse of the Holy Qur'an teaches you that Islam is not a religion, but it's the nature in which we were born. If you go to higher Masonry, they will ask you were you made a Mason, you'd better not tell them that you were made one; you've got to tell them that you have always been that. [3]

**Master
W. Fard
Muhammad**
Allah (God) In
Person

The Only Teacher
of
Elijah Muhammad
(Messenger of Allah)

THIS IS THE ONE
WHO SOUGHT
AND SAVED WE
WHO WERE LOST,
THUS

**THE
SAVIOUR**

FIRST THREE DEGREES IS THE BASE

The Holy Qur'an is a true and a righteous book all over the 196,940,000 square miles of earth and water. It's a true book. This is the book you should try and study. Don't go get Sale's translation; don't get no missionary of white peoples' translation of the Holy

Qur'an to look for truth, they will deceive you. They don't want you to be Muslims.

As you have proof of that today, you'll be persecuted, you'll be sent to prison again and again for accepting Islam, that's the truth. Of course, you go for accepting Christianity, as I told you, they, by nature are made to be against you. You could be there best follower, that don't make any difference. As along as you're a Blackman that's it; they are your enemy.

The Bible and the Holy Qur'an is referring to you and me if we sum up the teachings of all three scriptures, the Torah, the Gospel and the Holy Qur'an, they all refer to you and I. Using other peoples history to teach you of your own. Think over it my friend.

The poor lost member of the aboriginal Black Nation has now been found and is now guided by God himself, so that the Bible's prophesy may be fulfilled; wherein, it say's in Ezekiel, "I will go after them; I will search for them, until I have found them; I will free them." right? "Even I myself, I will go and search for them."

A parable was made of Solomon; wherein, the great architect got killed after building a beautiful Temple. Here, Solomon [symbolically] acts as the God: He sends searchers for him to find where had he fallen dead at. The searchers, when they returned said, "We found him, but we could not raise him, he was so rotten that his flesh slipped off his bones if we tried to raise him; he had been dead a long time. Nevertheless, we found a sign of life from his grave growing up from his grave, we see a sign of life.

The Bible says: "Though dead, but yet shall he live." You must know the truth. "He's dead, but yet he shall live." Again, those that die in the Lord shall live again, hence forth," says the spirit. The spirit of prophecy is referring to a people who will lose the knowledge of themselves and of their God. But don't consider them to be absolutely hopeless, for they will live again; they will live again.

How was he killed? "The enemy killed him by knocking him in his head." So if he was struck in the head, this is the real place to kill the man. Solomon said, "I will go and see if I can help you raise him." He went himself to show them how to get a hold of a dead man. Regardless to how secret you made it, it is the truth. It symbolizes the real people of today. He showed the people how to raise this man, how to take hold of the dead, after they had taken him up out of the grave, he directed that the dead man to be buried under the Temple. Though taken East, they found him in the West. [4]

I say to you my friends, many have attempted to try to solve your problems. Many have come here trying to raise you; you were too dead here. They couldn't raise you, but now the Father has come. The King of Peace has come and He has taught me [Elijah

Muhammad] how to get a hold of you. He said to me, "You must rise for the time is at hand." You must rise, it is written, look in your own Bible, it is time. The Bible teaches you itself that it is time that the dead should arise. "Stand him up, put him on the square, turn his face back to his people and to his native land, then he will be upright, then he will be forever successful from then on. Take him up."

While they were searching for the body, they heard someone in the bushes groaning. Those who had killed that fine architect was groaning and moaning; they were in agony over committing such evil. "Woe to me that I have ever brought such man here. I'm sorry, I'm sorry, but if your problems are not solved, America will say, "Woe to us for ever bringing such people as this to us, and for our evils that we have did against them."

I will tell you of that which I know for myself. I have had priests to come to me and say, "I'm sorry." He said, "We feel that we have mistreated you all and we would like to do something about it." But the time is right that you must rise.

Poor Marcus Garvey, a hard working man, he wanted so see you into your own, trying to buy ships to take you back to your own, which wasn't necessary. And if you're not given up and put back into your own land and among your own people, your stay here will not be doing any good to America. No, No, and the wise man of America knows that; for God himself have found you and God himself is after you and He's not going to let America rest nor will He let you rest until He has put you back into your place. Go after your own, seek your own God, seek your own religion, the religion of peace, you are a most beloved people. God just loves you, because you are nothing and He want to make something out of you. It is not that you are so great; no, you're nothing. It is not that you are so good, no you are evil yourself, but God just want to fulfill that which He put in the mouth of His prophet: that He would come after you after 400 years of enslavement and He would take you back and put you in your own native land. The world knows that you are the only people that don't know it, but I'm telling you.

Once I was a Mason too until I became a Muslim, I was a Mason. You must remember that the Holy Qur'an teaches that a Muslim or Moslem is the brother of the Muslim. You must remember the scripture or the rituals that they use concerning a lost architect, think over it. If we are studying that and learn what it means and who it actually really is, then I say you are wise. You must remember my friend, that these things all now has come to light.

There is a prophesy in the Bible that "He," meaning God, will send His Angels, send His people, from the East to gather you from the West. A Saviour has been born. "I will go after him, even I; I will search for him until I find him. When I find him, I'm going to take him back to his own people. He reached out and made a prophecy against the fall Israel: "I'm going to plant it on the hills, on the mountains of Israel." Don't look for earth, it's the rulers and the authority of that nation: the mountains of Israel. Israel [was] "voted" up as rulers of the people. "I'm going to mount you up and make you the ruler of self and others. I'm going to search for them." They have to be searched for, why? "An enemy has them and the enemy is hiding them. The enemy calls them by his name. They don't know Me. They are not wise as a donkey: the donkey knows his master, but My people do not know Me." Think over it. "I'm going to search for them; for an enemy has them and an enemy is hiding them. "They don't know Me, because the enemy didn't teach them of Me. They don't go in their own peoples' names; they don't pray the prayer of their people; they don't turn their faces toward the East; they don't spread out their hands to Me as I teach them. I must go after them; I must save them from such people." What are going to do with such people? "I'm going to turn them over to their own kind. I'm going to choose them; they're going to be My people; I'm going to make for Myself a Nation."

Who could or who should be any happier than you and me, that a Saviour was designed to come to save us. What are we in trouble with? "The time has come, as I give it to Abraham, that I'm going to judge that people, where they have been, who kept us slaves for 400 years. I'm going after them. I'm going to free them [blacks] again and I'm going to judge that people.

I'm going to announce judgment and death to them, because they have destroyed My people. They have robbed them; they have spoiled them; they have blinded them; they can't see all the way.

It is time that you wake up. Stop going down to the beer garden drinking your stomach full of intoxicating beer, going on cutting the silly act. Stop ordering hot liquids to drink to make yourself a worse fool. Stop taking your hard earned dollars wasting them up into liquor and beer that will turn you crazy and make you throw all of your money out into the streets and right back in the hand of the thief. Stop trying to buy expensive cars with only $50 a week income or $75 dollars a week income and the car note is $75 a month or $100 a month and you don't make but $50 or $75 a week, and your house rent is $75 or $100 a month. Not to mention your clothes, your food, your gas that you have to buy, which costs you .30 or .35 cents a gallon or more [speech made in 1959], you don't think of that. My friend you are too extravagant with such little, you a like the book says, you are a prodigal son. Prodigal means something that is extravagant, wasteful. We are too wasteful with nothing, no land whatsoever. You don't have no home here. Millions of us here don't even own enough land to produce enough food to feed us in peace. That's right. We don't own enough land to produce enough food feed 17 million mouths with black-eyed peas, and yet we are so rich that if we are given $75 a week or $50 a week; we can buy $5,000

Cadillac and sleep in it at night. We are too rich, we are too wasteful, we are too ignorant.

I say my friend wake up. We can't be satisfied with a $50 suit if the merchant shows us a $105 or $110 suit. If we don't have $110, if he says that we can pay little on it a week or so, OK. We sell our lives as slave for a $110 suit or $150 suit when we could have bought three or four suits for that. No my friend, that is wrong. We will never be anybody like that. I don't care if you go to paradise, you could soon break paradise if your going to live like that. Don't be like that. You are fascinated by the wealth of the rich man. These people are rich, they own the country, they own the money, they own the house you live in, they make your shoes you wear, they make the socks you wear, they make the pants you wear, the shirt you wear, the tie you put on your neck, they make the hat you put on your head, you sit down and don't make nothing.

They sawed and built your home, sawed the timber. They go and dig mug and burn brick to build you a home, you pay them for it. You could do a little of that, go buy you some muddy land dig up some mud, make you some bricks yourself, they teach you how to make a brick, but you're too rich, let them make it and I'll pay 10 or 15c a brick for it. You have too much money. Your roof falling in, you won't go up there and patch it, let him patch it, that's no good. Where are you going to build a nation out of yourself being that lazy? We are actually too lazy to do anything for ourselves.

And yet say, "You don't build me a house, you patch my roof, he don't put a lock on my door, man can't you do something for yourself?"

We must first find our own faults before we pile too many on the other fellow. We know the other fellow is guilty of all the many things that he should not have done that he did do; yet, you and I are not so innocent ourselves. We also are guilty for not doing for self. Get $10,000, sit down and play it on the horses like a millionaire, that's a millionaire's way. He doesn't have nothing to do with his money. He sits there and bet on racing horses out there, to see which one runs the fastest. He got money to throw away. Here you come up with 10 cent wanting to put it on the line. You loose your dime, that's all of it, but if he loose his $10,000 dollars, he has 10,000 more. It's a sin. Lets get together and do something about it.

I'm happy to say that he has been found due West. He must be restored; he must be taken back in the Temple of his own. The Temple that he was the architect of, he must be carried home. So I'm happy to say to you that all of these things is now come true in your own history. You are the answer to it all. You are Hiram Abif yourself. Yes sir, you are the one. You are the one that has been hit in the head, and it takes a long time for that head to heal. You are the one. You are the one that needs to be stood up. I say my friend you are the one that has the blindfold on. You are the one that ought to be crying for light and more light, but you are not, you're reaching for the blindfold. Stand up my friend for self and know that you're in the day that you must be separated from the people that you have known for the last 400 years. God doesn't lie; He doesn't allow his prophets to lie. It is written and it must be fulfilled, you must go back to your own.

I think the white people here have done a great thing for you and I. They have not driven you out of the country. They have tried to give you jobs. They have tried to feed you when you didn't have nothing to do, is that right? That's the truth. Give credit where it's due. They're still trying to feed you and you're out of work today. Look at the unemployment line around on the streets. They are out there now by the hundreds is that right? Don't have no work to do, but yet won't go to your own. It is like the book said Lazarus was: he just wouldn't leave the rich man's gate. He stayed there until the rich man died himself.

I say my friend, I have God on my side to bring you into a better condition. I have God on my side to bring you into a land of your own, a home of your own where you won't be giving other people a headache in their home and where you won't have a headache trying to find a home where there is no home for you.

This is the end of the white man's world. It could be the end of the Blackman's world if he wants to sit down and do nothing. Naturally you will soon come to an end if you don't do something for yourself. That is if no one else is not doing it for you. As I told you three or four years ago in the paper, that you cannot always depend on the white people to carry you. But you didn't believe it. Now the day is fast coming that he's about to tell you, he soon will tell you, "I just can't carry you, that's all, don't have nothing for you to do". And if he tells you that, what can you say? "Well I helped make the bread for you, now you don't want to give me none". But brother, if he tells you to go for yourself, that you are free, now get on out and look over this earth for a living for yourself - can you blame him? Will you blame an old mule that you open the locked gate and tell that mule, "There is green grass out there mule - go eat, help yourself," and that mule will not go out of that lot to eat, but still stand there licking the trough, it will make you angry with the mule. [5]

ELIJAH'S LIGHT IS WHAT YOU CRAVE AND SEEK!

In reading a book in Washington Congressional Library on Ancient Masonry, I had to laugh sometimes to see how we have been fooled. And now you'll get their highest degree in that order that no white man would ever teach you.

If we bring to you (I'm talking about the disbelievers and hypocrites), if we bring to you that Flag and tell you that is our sign or emblem, you that have studied degrees in Masonry should not hesitate to come over, because we give you more than what the devil has given you. The brothers, Fruit of Islam (FOI) are men who have learned more about Masonry than you. Your masonry has included the history of your slavery, but you don't know it. Your first three (3) degrees takes you into your slavery. Those three degrees there, they are the answer to your slavery, if you understand. But not understanding them, as the white man would not teach you the theology inside of it, it makes you dumb to even that which you actually own. I don't like to call you such names, but it's an easy answer to the truth of it. You look, the ignorant among you, look at that [Flag of Islam] and laugh at it, because he's ignorant of the truth of it, and he doesn't know what he's doing. He'll smile at his old stars and stripes; he calls it "Old Glory." If I were you, I'd change the name and say it's "Old Hell."

I'm positive that if you would let me teach you, you'll go out sticking out your little chest. It will make you feel like sticking your chest out, but I say don't act proud; be humble and yet commanding. If we bring to you the Sun Moon and Star and you laugh at it, criticize it, and say you don't want it and say that you'd rather have a made square of the devil and that, that's enough for you to get by, you're only wishing to become recognized by the devil, not by you and your people. That is why you go and join up with them in every society that you think he will let you in. You want to be his equal, be recognized and respected by him. He didn't make his society or societies to make you his equal. He robbed you of money to be called one of them. He doesn't like to call you a "brother" in no society. Now, before we will tell him that we will accept him calling us "brothers," he tries to call us "brothers." Many white people out there call us "brothers" or refers to us as "the brothers," because we have the truth and the right act, in our right position of the square. We don't do this for form or fashion; no; it is the truth. If we say that we are "on the square with you," that don't mean that we're just saying that because the sign is a Square. No; we say that because we are "the Square" ourselves. Not that we make a sign to go by, we're the Square, and we are the Star, and we are the Moon. While you do these things according to his teaching, just for the respect of the whites who are one. They are getting recognition of it in America and then Australia and into Europe. This is just a act that they have for you to buy to get among them, and Freemasonry, even in itself, does not take you any further than Australia and into Europe. But this [Flag of Islam] takes you all over the Earth.

I want you to wake up and know yourself to be people of the first order, not of the last order, but of the first order. We are to respect each other as brothers and not as enemies. We are to respect our woman as our mother. I say my friend, this means that we have to love each other. We can't do these things if we hate each other. That's why we are very careful with you. The devil has put poison in your mind against self and love of yourself for him, and hoping you can be like him. Hope that you don't be like him. These people were made for hellfire. They were made to live only to a certain time. He tells us himself. Some places he goes that the children of the natives see him and say "There goes a foreign devil." They know him better than you. A real devil is one that is made by nature of evil; his very nature, the material which he's made, I do not use the word create, because he is not from the creation, he's a made man that our scientist, Yakub made here 6,000 years ago. We have been on this earth every since it was created.

Blackman remember you are the father of creation. Blackman remember that no white man can dispute with the one who said it, Elijah. He can't dispute with me; I'm a God taught man; I am a God raised man. I wear this on my head (Sun, Moon and Star), but we tell the white man to wear it publicly, but once a year. You know why he can't wear it over once a year? Because he has nothing to do with the making of this. The Blackman made this fez. What I mean, the Sun, Moon and Star. The white man knows nothing about the creation of such planets. This is why I want to teach you the theology of it. Many things in the universe, many things on earth of human beings and of life of any kind, I'm here to tell you what Allah has taught me of it, not what I know, it is Allah, The One Who has taught me and I don't think you will be able to make Him out [as telling] other than the truth. [6]

TRADE IN "OLD GLORY" FOR A STARRY CROWN

You have had 400 years here to listen to the slave master teaching you how to stay a slave to him. I have not been here 4 hours, so I think you ought to listen to me [Elijah Muhammad] for a little while.

If a man coming to you, in your presence, put such signs [before] them with such readings as that [Actual Facts Board], I warn you, you'd better listen to him. What does that mean? He's defying any world outside of the world of God, Allah to tangle with Him on the truth of what he have on that board. You cannot take these writings that is on that board and use it unless you are a Believer, regardless to the wisdom that's in it, you can not use it and be successful unless you are a believer in it. The truth that the man hanging on a tree under your Slave-master's flag, you believe he's right, you want your flag to be his "Old Glory," but I say, what has "Glory," "Old Glory," the stars and the stripes, given to you and me, but what you see, the victim there hanging on a limb.

Every night and day you listen over the radio and you see on the T.V., he's chasing a poor Blackman to take his life away from him. Under that beautiful red background with a Star and with a Crescent [Flag of Islam], you don't see over here no Islamic people chasing each other. When you believe in Islam, all the world of Islam will recognize and respect you. They will fight for you, they will die for you.

We [who] proclaim those same stars and that moon and that red background that represents the Sun. What does that represent? The Sun is a ball of fire and a light. And the Sun, we all live in it, we respect it, and out of the Sun comes our food, out of the Sun comes our direction. I say to you my believing brothers and my disbelieving brothers, take a look at it. That's our Flag [sun, moon and star] and your Flag is a Flag of mixed mystery, blue, red and white], ours is one solid background, red. The Sun and Moon is there together and the Stars associated with that same Crescent, showing the world that we have laid hold on the greatest instruments of heaven and earth to condemn any disputer who will attack us.

We use to buy it [Masonry], trying to make friendship with Satan. We go and buy that Crescent put it on our coat, laughing and looking at him when he passes, to as good as say to him, "See I have the Crescent on me; you should take me for your brother." We gave it to him after he had shown us that he could act like us from 35 or 40 or 50 years. We let him wear our Crescent, that's ours. The red and the Crescent over it, that's ours. He can take his mystery [American flag] for himself, but if he wears that [Flag of Islam], look at him again, he worked for that, he didn't get that so easy.

[American flag] got blue, which is an untrue color; you have many stars there. It takes all of those stars to try to justify something. It shouldn't be done like that. We got one star, which justifies [us], which represents all the stars, is ours. There are six stripes of red [in the American flag], not a solid background of red, because the red represents freedom, and he doesn't give freedom - only to those who are able and wealthy. If you're able to buy it from him, he'll give you freedom. [7]

[My followers are wearing it on their heads], because now God is turning over to the slaves, Blackman, the Universe, and that they are within their right, to put it on their head, because it's theirs.

If you don't see the white mason wearing it but once a year, you wonder then, wow, why we don't wear it along with them once a year. No, we're the father of it. So, if the father is going to lay his emblem aside to go along with the non-owner, then the father is doing this either for trying to make acquaintance with him in his own country, or the father is just laying his down for a certain time.

Today we are able to wear our Fez, which represents the universe. But white people don't do this, they wear them once a year in some kind of turnout, because this is not his, that's why he doesn't wear it. He's a man put in the universe for a time, and at the end of that time, he gets out of our house. If he doesn't get out, we'll throw him out.

The world or not [necessarily] this world, but the Heavens and the Earth belong to black people, and this is why this teachings has come to you; it is to acquaint you into the knowledge of your own. [8]

THE GREAT SHAME OF AMERICA

In a Small monthly paper printed in Morris Plains, N.J., in the language of true Moslem Shriners, the following appeared in the January 1959 issue:

It says: "The greatest shame upon the escutcheon of America: Its treatment of Negroes. These Americans are here, because their forefathers were ruthlessly kidnapped in Africa, herded into suffocating ships, chained, beaten and sold into slavery."

"Much white blood is in the veins of American Negroes. Southern aristocrats had children by Negro women (and are still getting them by the Negro woman). Union occupation armies fathered many children by Negro women. Those fierce racists opposing the inevitable dawn of justice for Negroes ironically are fighting their own flesh and blood."

"These persecuted descendants of slaves go right on (like fools) defending the democracies of (white) Africans. Ralph Bunche, Negro Nobel Prize winner, UN Under-Secretary, refused an invitation to become

U.S. Assistant Secretary of State, because Washington D.C. had jim-crow laws."

"American Negroes dress American, talk American, live American, die American. Over a million Negro soldiers took up arms for American in World War II (some 400,000 fought for America in 1917)."

"Dead Negro Americans are buried with white soldiers on every Revolutionary War battle field, only to be denied justice by the white soldiers of America (the Government). The first (fool) American patriot killed in the Boston Massacre was a Negro. The first (fool) woman to fight in the American Army was a Negro who disguised herself as a man to fight for America's independence."

"Negroes paid the crimson cost of liberty at Antietam, Vicksburg, San Juan Hill, the Argonne, Chateau Theirry, Leyte Gulf, the Ardennes Bulge, Aizio Beachhead, Iwo Jinna, Hungnam, the Yalu and Inchon Reservoir."

"Every other tie on the roadbed of the Union Pacific and the DL&W is the worked-out, sweated-out body of a Negro. The fiery tongues of molten iron pouring out of American Negro workers."

"And without recrimination, They sang "Swing Low Sweet Chariot" and "Come Down Sweet Jesus" as they lifted and existed on next to nothing, lived in unsanitary firetraps, ghettoed, jim-crowed.

"Negro Americans can be the deciding factor in world power. Today two-thirds of the world are "people of color." It further takes a snap at Masonry, which the Negroes buy, seeking justice and respect as a man and as the brother of man in these words: "If Masonry is for light, then there can be no lampshade on its light. If the brotherhood of man is all-inclusive-not a cruel joke-then Masonry must be honest with itself or go down as history's great mockery."

The So-Called Negroes are tools in the hands of their enemies and were made blind, deaf and dumb by their enemies (the slave masters) when they were babies; yet, they think their devil enemies are their friends. They give their lives for their enemies to be free to keep them subjects, beaten, lynched, raped and killed. They help the white devils destroy their own women by giving her all the freedom she wants in their homes, stores, restaurants, hotels, offices, factories, farms and baby-sitters. They strip her before the devils and ask the devils to accept her, and she foolishly accepts the devil to destroy her family's morals and to spot her children with the devil's blood, even after having knowledge that the same white man will not give her and her men folk justice in any court.

Negro Masons, do not buy the white man's Masonry. There is no brotherhood there for you. It is only a farce of justice. Come and accept the real Islam, the Muslim. I [Elijah Muhammad] am the door. I will let you in. For our slavery, sweat, blood and life, one-half of America is not enough as pay.

MOSLEM SHRINERS

Before the coming of Allah, Islam was sold to the so-called Negroes in a secret order or society called the Masons. This order is made up of thirty-three (33) degrees and it is sold by degrees. If a member is eligible and able to pay for all the degrees he may do so, but only those who take the thirty-third (33rd) are called Moslem Shriners.

Though real Islam is not practiced in this secret order, it is made a farce. The first three (3) degrees are the base of the whole; they are full of significance pertaining to the robbery and murder of a valuable member of a significant Temple, and a friend of the wisest King that ever lived. (Left, John Grant State Senator, Tampa, Florida; Right, Gerald Ford, Former President USA, Rancho Mirage, California.

Upper Left clock wise, Buzz Aldrin, Astronaut o Laguna Beach, California; Glen Ford, Actor, Beverl Hills, California; Roy Clark, Country & Wester singer, Tulsa, Oklahoma; and Ernest Borgnine Actor, Beverly Hills, California

ISLAM FREE

You do not have to buy Islam; it is free. Islam is the salvation of the Black Nation, and the only way out for the so-called American Negroes. Islam means submission to the will of Allah (God).

What greater religion is there than a religion that demands us to submit to the will of Almighty God (Allah)? The number one (1) principle of belief in Islam is the belief in One God. Is not this the teachings of the Prophets of old, Abraham, Moses, Jesus, and Muhammad?

Endnote

---

[1] Radio Broadcast "The War of Armageddon."

[2] Theology of Time Audio, June 11, 1972

[3] Theology of Time Audio, June 18, 1972

[4] Saviour's Day 1967, Audio

[5] Saviour's Day 1959, Audio

[6] Theology of Time Audio June 11, 1972

[7] Theology of Time Audio August 27, 1972

[8] Theology of Time Audio June 11, 1972

Send Catalog Request To:

Secretarius Publications
PO Box 162412
Atlanta, GA 30321
770 907-2212
email:
admin@elijahmuhammadbooks.com

Wholesale rates also available.

NOTES

The earth is 196,940,000 square miles of earth and water.

NOTES

NOTES